# Feel the Paint

A sound approach to painting with young children

Garage 22
Randers, Denmark

www.garage22.dk

ISBN 978-87-972520-0-0

# Contents

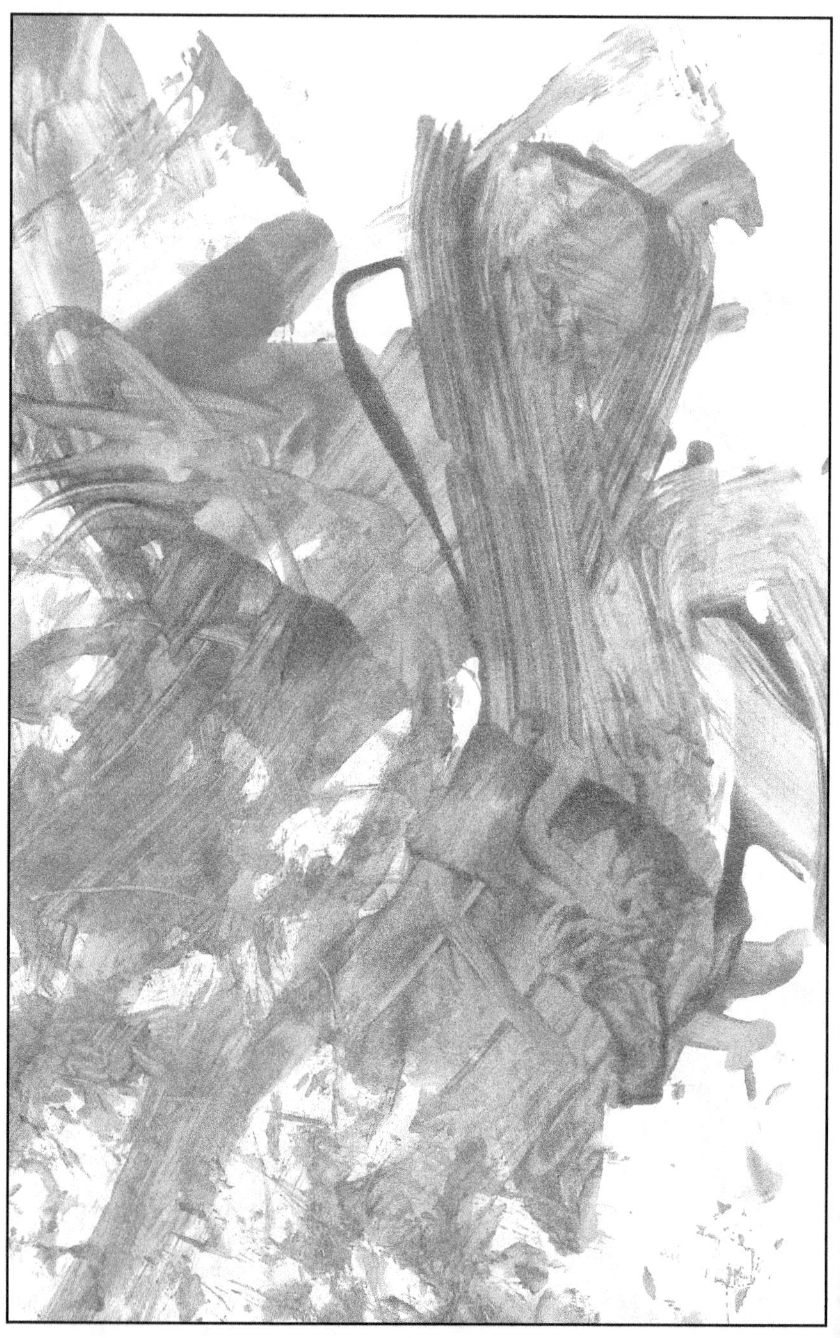

# Oh my goodness, there's paint everywhere!

Whether you're a professional working with children or a seasoned parent, you'll probably have found yourself in a messy situation at some point with paint, glue or glitter all over the place. That sticky stuff gets into socks and curtains and ponytails as if by magic. It really does happen to all of us!

Even though it's usually fixed with a bit of soap and water and the kids helping along with the cleaning, we sometimes ask ourselves why we even bother.

In this book you'll find examples of painting and drawing activities to inspire you to get creative with your own children or the children in your kindergarten or school. Sometimes it's messy and loud and sometimes it's very subtle. You'll also find different aesthetic learning strategies and approaches to children's creative development. Furthermore the book addresses the importance of actively supporting that development as a vital part of growing up as a human being.

"But I'm not a creative person! I can't even draw a stick figure!"

Creative endeavours shouldn't be reserved for your artistic colleagues or your imaginative spouse. No matter where you think you are on a creative scale, you're more than able to paint with children.

Just read on…

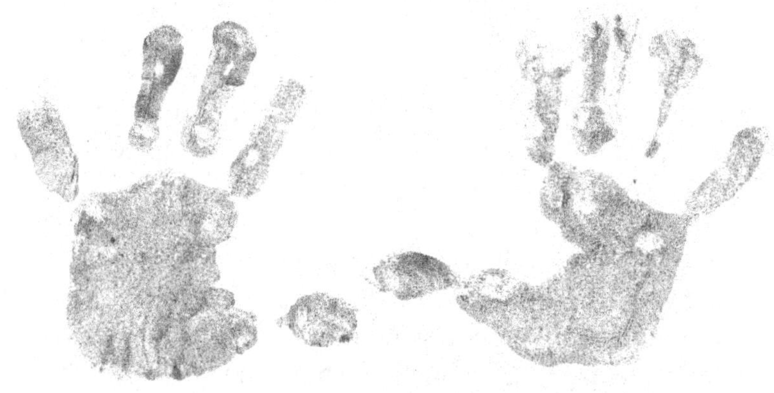

# Kindergarten Cop Painter

I put together this book to share my experiences, thoughts and opinions on creative activities with children. Along the years and during my education I fell upon theories and studies, which I found helpful in trying to understand how children grow as imaginative and resourceful humans.

I haven't taken an academic approach to the development theories in 'Feel the Paint'. Instead I've focused on a somewhat more practical approach and suggested a certain mindset when dealing with children and paint.

I'm trained as a kindergarten teacher, a BA in Early Childhood Education and Preschool Teaching in Denmark, and have a decade of professional experience with kids from zero to six years old. In this book I'm dispensing some of that accumulated knowledge wherever appropriate.

Besides working with children I'm also a visual artist working primarily in oils, acrylics and watercolours. I've been fortuned to be able to combine my professional life with my artistic interests – not just in doing art and exhibits with the kids, but also in everyday life situations when discovering colours and new shapes crawling around on all fours with the toddlers.

# Splashing paint around doesn't get you a college degree – or does it?

What does it mean to be creative? If you ask around, you might get answers like 'able to draw something that looks like something' or perhaps 'able to come up with a picture from imagination'. Among colleagues in a school or day-

care centre that definition could be common, but creativity is more than that.

Take a situation with four children sitting at a table. They are given paper and crayons. Three of them are drawing nice flowers and stick figures while the fourth is rolling up a piece of paper and shoots crayons out of it like a blowgun. Who's the most creative around that table?

Being creative is also about the ability to think outside the box and crafting up things, no one has ever seen before. Seeing what's in front of you and putting colours and stuff together in a new way. Creativity is believed to be the source of growth and prosperity for the human species in the future, and lateral thinking, innovation and entrepreneurship is what the corporate world wants to greater and greater extent.

Research results suggest that creative work enhances the understanding of mathematics and abstract science. When you help the child to experience and gain trust in its own creation abilities, it benefits the child in the long run, but please remember that creativity and ingenuity isn't something anyone can force. Just as any psychologist would say you can't force a child's development. You can guide in a certain direction and be aware of what impulses you give the child, but you can't rush the progress.

More about impulses later…

Example

# Art birds

Finger-painting activity

Age:        1-3 approx.
Group:   1-4
Purpose:  Experience wet paint with fingers and hands

Place the children at the table wearing aprons. Once the paint is on the hands it gets everywhere – face, hair, chair, you. Using modern acrylic paint usually ensures non-toxic materials that are fairly easy to wash away. But have damp washcloths and paper towels ready before you begin.

Children below the age of two or so are prone to examine the world with their senses only, mostly orally. Their level of reflection is generally somewhat limited to linking basic physical needs: Hunger –> Cry –> Food. Putting their hands into the paint and then leaving a trace on the paper is a similar, very tactile way of experiencing the world around them.

Show them how it's done. This activity isn't about true artistic expression. It's fine if the kids copy exactly what you do. Dip your fingers and make some bold strokes on the paper. Then set aside, wash your hands quickly and let the children play with the paint under your supervision and guidance.

Some children don't like to get their fingers sticky or dirty. This could be related to parents and other primary caregivers who tend to wash the children's hands for hygienic reasons the second they get oatmeal or sand or a bugger on them. Painting with fingers could cause some kids to shy away from the activity, so you should have a couple of brushes on stand by to help the children back in. Once they see their friends use their hands, they might be convinced.

When the paint is dry you can add beaks and eyes or possibly legs and feet with a black marker to gently finish the 'art birds' without disturbing the unique expression of each painting. If you're running a theme of something completely different like Pets or Trees or Family, shake it up and adjust accordingly.

**Do you want ketchup with that?**

I once had a group of two-year-old boys and girls doing finger-painting. I used ordinary plates to put the paint on, one colour on each. One of the girls saw me squish out a red substance from a bottle onto the plate before I pushed it across the table to her. As soon as I looked away she put her finger into it and tasted it with her tongue.

The paint was harmless... It was a very small amount... The girl was fine!

# Goals can be dangerous

If you are a homeschooling parent or a professional working with children, you probably got a certain goal or curriculum that you aim for. They're more or less strict guidelines to what the children must learn and must be able to do. In places like the United Kingdom and the United States there's a tradition of this kind of goal setting throughout the education system involving a lot of tests along the way from kindergarten to college and beyond. This very scholastic method is also known as the Anglo-Saxon or Curriculum tradition.

In contrast there's the Continental tradition, mostly based on an open, experimental learning didactic, in which the children learn by themselves fuelled by interest and curiosity with the adult as a resourceful guide.

So why is it dangerous to set a goal for your creative activity with your children? They do have to learn something, right?

Well, no. If you set a goal, it means you have to be able to measure success. A test will show with a high degree of certainty if a child knows how to multiply or read a text. But measuring a child's self-worth and growing understanding of the world is much less accurate to say the least. You can set goals, but the Continental tradition is more open to other equally valuable outcomes such as the ability to see the interconnectiveness of all things, social and personal development, lateral thinking and a general belief in your own ability to act.

The danger of a goal too specific is the learning possibilities you potentially miss out on. It turns your focus more on the finishing line instead of the process itself.

**Dead mouse principle**

I'm walking through the forest with a group of children. We're on our way to a specific place in the forest where I know we can find certain mushrooms. All morning we've talked about mushrooms and I'm thinking the kids should draw their own watercolour mushrooms when we get back.

On the path we come across a dead mouse. The children are very excited and curious about it. We stop and carefully examine the dead mouse. I ask them what they think happened to the mouse, where it lived and so on. The kids are 100% focused on the animal and I take the opportunity to adjust my objective for the day.

We forget the mushrooms and explore and learn about food chains and the forest eco system instead. I use the children's interest to my advantage and to support their development as human beings.

The process itself is very much the centre of the Continental tradition, and in Scandinavian kindergartens the focus is generally on children's play. They're learning stuff through play and exploration in interaction with other kids. Studies show that this really goes on for the rest of life, but it's primarily true for children. They feel the paint and reach new insights so to speak.

However with globalization the two traditions are influencing each other, and these years Scandinavia sees an increase of tests in the educational system. This also seems to be a result of New Public Management in both schools and day care centres with a higher level of control and tests in the name of economic efficiency.

Example

# Portrait discovery

Drawing and self awareness activity

Age:      4-10 approx.
Group:    2-20 (in pairs)
Purpose:  Practising basic drawing skills, perception of
          difference in details, developing refined sense
          of self

**Part 1**

Let the kids draw themselves. Give the youngest ones a
good start by talking about facial expressions and ask them
to draw their own face. Let the older ones decide if they
draw faces, half or full figures. Remember to write names
on all the portraits.

**Part 2**

Then set the portraits aside and give the children a mirror
and a fresh sheet of paper. Ask them to draw themselves
again. This time around they're warmed up, but the sud-
den presence of a mirror might throw some kids off a bit.
Confronted with an actual representation of what you're
supposed to reproduce can be challenging.

**Part 3**

The third time around you ask the children to draw each
other. Team them up two by two and let them work at each
other's faces one at a time.

---

**TIPS**

Using pens instead of brushes means more accuracy
and attention to the details that makes us look different
and the same.

It's common to see a child beginning his portrait with
a head that's way too small to fit eyes and nose and
mouth into. The entire figure will end up microscopic
on the large piece of paper. Give him a new piece
right away and apologies for not showing him the size
of the head beforehand. Show it on a different paper
and let him know that he didn't do anything wrong.

---

**Part 4**

Exhibit all the portraits by putting the three version of the
same kid next to each other. Talk about some of the fea-
tures that perhaps a child didn't see herself but her friend
did. Look for the positive aspects and try to keep the conversation encouraging and focus on both differences and
similarities.

# Establish a platform for creative exploration

Studies show that children and adults alike are more creative and prone to explore new possibilities when they stand
on a safe platform. This means a safe environment where
they feel comfortable both physically and emotionally.
A safe platform is the room you're familiar with, but it's
also the security of knowing you can trust the people
around you. A safe platform is an environment where
mistakes aren't frowned upon, not by other kids and not by
colleagues.

**Home Away Home principle**
When teaching kids about creative art forms or simply
introducing your child at home to a new aesthetic concept,
it's a good idea to apply the Home Away Home principle.
By doing so you take advantage of the safe platform and the
children's natural curiosity.

The definition of *home* and *away* could in some cases literally mean 'at home where you live' and 'away on a school
trip'. But in general the terms are to be understood as *home
on a safe platform* (a known environment such as the class-
room or the playground) and *away from the platform to
explore a new subject territory*.

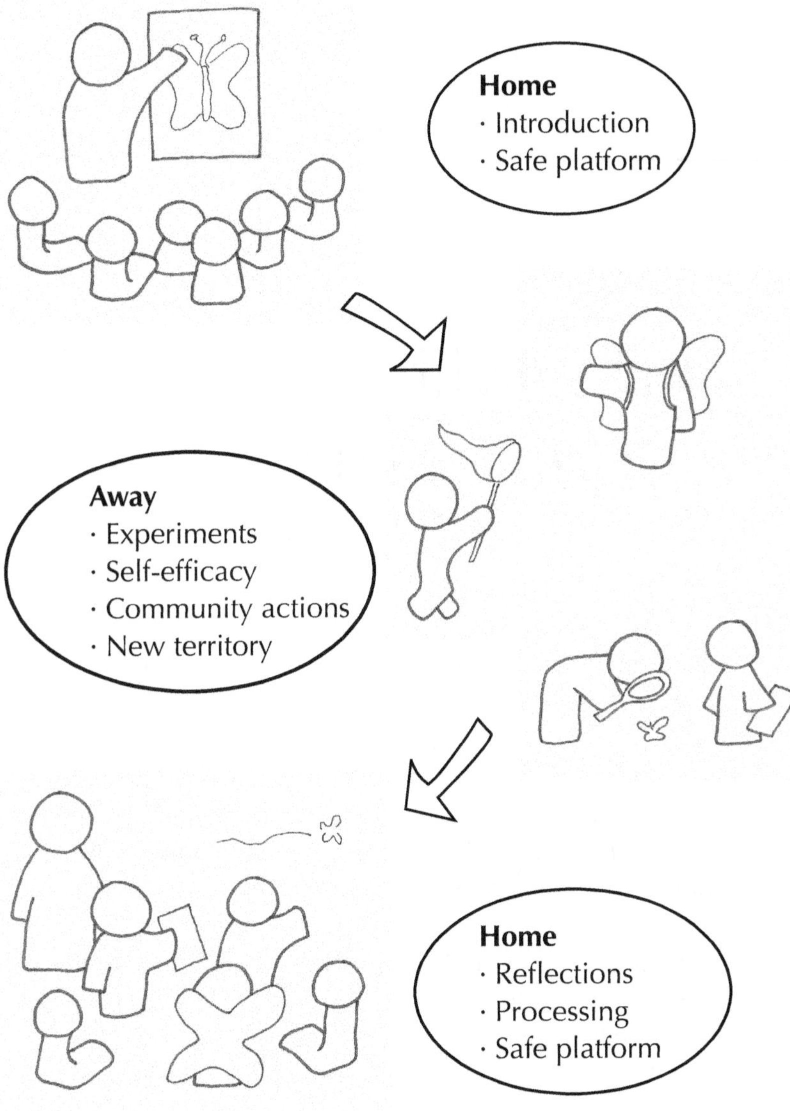


The Home Away Home principle can be applied to all sorts of activities and subject matters – not just visual expressions. You take the theory out into the world and carry the experience back home with you.

Example

# Paint from life
# – no pulse required

Perception and painting activity

Age:       3-6 approx.
Group:    4-7
Purpose: Practising basic drawing and painting skills,
            developing perception

When you tell kids to draw an elephant, they probably say:
"We can't!" But if you put a toy elephant on the table, look
at it together and talk about the different shapes, the task
suddenly seems possible.

Painting and drawing from life adds a new perspective to
your creative activities. By observing and then reproduc-
ing, the children will get a set of basic drawing skills that
they'll use over and over later on when they draw from
imagination.

Place an object on the table where everybody can see it.
Talk about what you see. Listen to the children's observa-
tions. What shapes do they see?

Begin drawing alongside the children. Everyone draws the same feature – the big round shape of the body for instance. Wait for all to finish the first step. Then proceed to the head or the legs. Again wait for everybody to draw each step.

Be careful to draw your own elephant as simply as possible even if you can do it much more accurately. The children must be able to see your drawing at each step and say:
"Hey, I can do that!"
Keep to the almost abstract shapes and remember to share your little mistakes: "Oops, the head on my elephant ended up very, very small. Never mind that!"

You're essentially being a good example by being a bad example.

---

**Keep it shorty pants!**

As young children have limited attention spans, try and keep an activity like this to 30 minutes at most. If some of them hurry to draw the subject and leave the table before you all finish, let them do that. They'll disturb the rest of the children less if they're allowed to play instead. Next time they might be more motivated to follow your speed in the process.

# Welcome to the art studio

The educational philosophy from Northern Italy, Reggio Emilia, is based on the image of a child with strong potential for development that grows in relations with others. One of the concepts in this popular pedagogy movement is the idea of *the room as the third educator*. It's believed that you're one educator, the approach to teaching and guidance you use is another educator, and the room or surroundings is the third educator. The interaction between the three is essential.

The physical surroundings and the way you decorate and divide into smaller "rooms within the room" send different signals. A day care centre for instance is therefore typically designed with certain bases or stations: A play kitchen, a reading corner, a carpet with printed tracks for toy cars etc. They each send a specific vibe, a signal of what to expect and strong suggestions of different types of play and interactions. It's the mood of a physical setting, the unspoken invitation to a certain activity.

It's the atmosphere gathered through all your senses. What it looks like, what it smells like, what it sounds like.

Surroundings could mean basic things like architectural structures, lighting and the colour of the walls, but also a micro space that you create with a child when you put down a small blanket in the middle of a busy room and have a two-person intimate tea party sharply defined by the edges of the blanket.

Using atmosphere consciously is a powerful tool when trying to motivate and capture a young audience in creative, visual activities. Having a dedicated art studio isn't for everyone, but at least you can make the art studio *space* appear on the table or the floor or in the park. Make sure to have things prepared and visible to the children from the beginning. It sends an important signal of creative energy and excitement to actually see the paint tubes and brushes and maybe the easel.

Easy access to materials such as colours, paper, glue, scissors etc. is also important for both the children and yourself. If you don't have a dedicated art studio, of course these materials must be put away when you're done with them, but how easy are they to get to? For you it must be easy in order to offer creative activities frequently. For both you and the kids it must be readily available and visible to inspire ideas. Even though crayons and papers are put away on a shelf, they still radiate an important atmosphere as long as they're visible and easy to get to.

An example of how the feel and expectations of a room can work against your intentions: One time I asked six four-year-olds to reflect upon my questions to them about different categories. I asked them: "Are you a boy or a girl?" and stuff like "Do you have siblings or not?" Although I did tell them to physically split into two groups for each question, they couldn't really concentrate on the activity because of the environment. I had chosen the "gym" room that had lots of mattresses on the floor, giant pillows, balls and soft slides. The kids were used to running around and playing in there, so that was their expectation based on experience. The strong suggestions, the atmosphere, of the room were simply too strong for them to ignore.

**Messy supply experiment**
Working with a group of 24 children in kindergarten my colleagues and I realized that their drawing skills were surprisingly poor. Even super simple shapes seemed difficult for the children. We set out to experiment with the access to materials, which had been more or less adult regulated until that point.

We made a small space available on a shelf in the children's eye level with plenty of cheap photocopy paper, ink markers, plastic covers, aprons and watercolour supplies. We introduced it to the kids and asked them to keep the supplies tidy.

The first couple of days were a bit messy. The children got water from the tap in the bathroom in small cups, which meant a lot of cleaning up, before they could even begin painting. The paper ran out pretty fast and had to be restocked, and the images they made were fast paced and often in mixed, murky brown.

After that, it settled down. The children began painting and drawing only when they actually felt like it – not just because the easy access was new and exciting. Water on the floor was rare, and when it happened, the kids learned to help each other clean up. The supply shelf was tidy and the images improved considerably over the course of only a few weeks. Stick figures emerged everywhere and beautiful pictures of crooked flowers and dogs with seven legs came to life in crisp and bright colours.

Example

# Journey from paintbrush to exhibit

Painting, framing and showing the artwork

Age:      1-99
Group:    1-99
Purpose: Knowing the ability to affect the world

Most of the creative projects and artworks the children
come up with should be on display. This is often a tradition
in school and other institutions, even at home when you
put drawings on the fridge.

We do this as adults not only because it pleases the children as they perceive the act of displaying itself as an
obvious appreciation of the thing they produced, but also
because the underlying psychological effects are driving the
children's development and sense of thriving and wellbeing.
A child in balance and positive thriving will grow and learn.

Danish professor Bente Jensen, Ph.D. defines four key factors when describing the sense of wellbeing:

1.	Feeling connected
2.	Being met with respect and recognition
3.	Being in development
4.	Taking control

When you arrange an exhibit, which can be as simple as sticking a drawing to the middle of the fridge with a magnet, you're meeting the child with respect and a recognition of the artwork by acting on it. The child learns that it can take control and affect its surroundings – that it has a place and belongs in the world.

This principle of wellbeing is applicable to adults as well…

As you probably know, it's important to be involved in the entire process from paintbrush to framing to hanging the pictures to designing the invites and to the actual exhibition. The kids will experience a meaningful sequence of actions and gain a stronger sense of ownership, belonging and pride in their work.

Invite the parents and the neighbours. Invite the press! Visual stories are the best, but remember also to show and tell the story of the process with photos and anecdotes from each stage of the artistic journey.

# Create an impulse

Working with aesthetic creations is a matter of turning
impressions into expressions. The impressions are basically
all the things that happen in the child's life including the
intentional and unintentional things, we as adults put in
front of the child. No one can say for sure what sparks new
ideas, but we can enable the child to act on them.

British creativity researcher and drama teacher Malcolm
Ross defined the different elements that go into creative
ability. They are: the Senses, Imagination, Craft skills and a
Medium into which the creativity can manifest itself. But
Ross also pointed to a playful atmosphere as a vital part, as
well as the importance of some sort of impulse.

An impulse occurs as a result of inner, emotional unbalance. Something that disturbs our image of the world or sets
a chain of thoughts into motion. A simple walk in the park
or listening to a new piece of music could ignite a firework
of impulses in the child. An example of a very intentional
influence is to give the children a specific object to look at
and draw from.

Unintentional influences that result in positive unbalance
and creative desire in the child could be the shiny colour of
the car outside the window, a new child in class, the smell

of cheese from your lunchbox or a really good time on the swing set.

It doesn't have to be mind-blowing experiences in order to create impulses.

Example

# Draw to scale

Drawing and painting different sized objects

Age:       5-10 approx.
Group:   1-10
Purpose: Learning about aspect ratio and comparison

This activity is great if you're having a fantasy theme of either Giants or Gnomes and Fairies or perhaps a focus on Children vs. Adults. It's all about aspect ratio and drawing something to look either big or small compared to the thing, you draw next to it.

For instance: Begin drawing a human figure with a perma-
nent marker. Let the face be roughly centred on the paper.
Now draw a flower next to the figure and make sure the top
of the flower nearly touches the top edge of the paper. Use
watercolour to finish the painting.

It trains the ability to look carefully at details of both very
big and very small subjects. The understanding of scale
and comparison might seem simple, but this is a good way
to introduce the concept to children, and it helps them to
position themselves in the physical world.

**TIP**
Suggest that the children paint themselves big and then
paint you in miniature next to them. Kids often find it
hilarious and could lead to a conversation of when and if
size matters. Is it easier to reach stuff when you're tall? Is it
always the tallest person who's in charge?

**Thoughts on praising your child's artwork**

It comes very natural to us as adults, and especially as parents, to almost auto-praise our kids when they've produced a drawing or stacked a towering bunch of Lego-blocks on top of each other. There's nothing wrong with praise, but we need to realize the difference between praise and recognition.

Praise is, roughly put, based on the achievement, the end product, and is perceived as a reward for producing something. Recognition is based more on the process and investment from the child. Where praise speaks to value, recognition speaks to self-esteem.

You recognise the child when you say things like: "I saw you worked a long time on this and you used a lot of different colours! Looking at your drawing makes me very happy!"

# Brainy girls and clever boys

Of course you already know this. There's more than one way to be intelligent. "I'm not very good at math, but I can build you a solid piece of furniture any day!"

This goes for children as well and makes it next to impossible to compare any two people on the planet. What does intelligence even mean and how does it relate to paint, glue and glitter?

On the question of defining intelligence, psychologist Howard Gardner has suggested looking at primarily eight different sub categories: Spatial, Naturalist, Musical, Bodily-kinaesthetic, Logical-mathematical, Interpersonal, Intra–personal and Linguistic intelligence. According to Gardner we're all a mix of these categories with more weight in some and less in others.

Logical-mathematical and linguistic intelligence is most valued in school and society in general. Encouraging children to paint and be creative strengthens their musical, intrapersonal and spatial areas of understanding. Spatial in this context means the ability to recognize and manipulate patterns on both large and tiny scales – visualizing the world in 3D, so to speak.

As mentioned in the beginning of the book, splashing paint around does not get you a college degree on its own, but it broadens your palette of ways to grasp and handle the world literally and mentally.

Professors Rita and Kenneth Dunn came up with a model of learning styles back in the 1970's, which is still widely accepted as a good overview of the ways human beings learn new things.

The model shows 20 different aspects or factors in learning styles. One of them is whether or not you're 'global' or 'analytical'. Studies have indicated that about 80% of children in kindergarten are naturally global, which means they benefit from knowing what an activity is about and what's expected of them before they begin. This could perhaps be achieved by beginning with telling a short story, showing an example of an end result or explaining why they need to do A before B. The more analytical inclined children prefer to do A first and then learn about B after that, one step at a time.

Both Dunn & Dunn and Gardner's approaches suggest useful methods of differentiating the way we teach.

> *"If the child is not learning the way you are teaching, then you must teach in the way the child learns."*
>
> -Rita Dunn

Example

# Paint a tree

Observation and interpretation

Age:      4-10 approx.
Group:   1-10
Purpose: Artistic freedom and realizing variations

Take a walk. Observe the different kinds of trees with the children and discuss variations in height, width, colour, shape and so on. Throw in a little science and use the right names if you know them.

Let each child pick its own tree. If possible, mark or remember that tree so you can return to it later and perhaps repeat the activity or just to make sure the tree is doing well.

Weather permitting, draw the trees on notepads or in sketchbooks. Talk to each child about what they like about their tree. It makes them focus on what it actually looks like and what makes it a bit different from all the rest. Make it clear however that it's perfectly fine to leave out a certain branch you dislike or maybe borrow the bird nest from your friend's tree.

Back home they paint the trees again, but this time on larger paper and go crazy with all the colours they'd like their trees and backgrounds to have. Remember, it's their trees, not yours.

Throw an exhibition: Welcome to the fantasy forest!

## TIP

Young children can have a hard time keeping watercolour on the right side of the line. Give them dark and medium colours for the trees in the foreground and let the images dry a bit. Then give them lighter colours for the background. This way it's okay to paint over the darker tree a bit as it will not really show.

# Connecting through drawing

Your relationship with each other plays a major part in how you can guide and motivate the child to positive development. Master in Educational Psychology Anna K. Andreasen has come up with a method to use a close personal connection to help the child grow.

Her concept translates into "Drawing-Talking method" and is a structured way of working on things like language, social skills, concentration and so on.

This isn't a thorough presentation of the concept, but you basically put a half hour or hour on the schedule each week where you sit down to draw with the child. Just the two of you in a room where you're not disturbed. You draw and talk.

The way you draw in the Drawing-Talking method is more specific however. Keeping it simple with plenty of paper and whatever pens or colouring devices the child prefers, you sit next to each other and let the child draw what it feels like. You mirror that drawing more or less while being interested in what it is and how the child does it. Slowly your conversation can turn into a direction or subject matter that you find beneficial, but it's a delicate balance.

Using this method is about making the child comfortable in the room, in the repeated time structure with you, feeling free to draw anything. Don't force the conversation. You can mirror the child's drawing and sometimes add a little something extra to your version. As you sit next to each other, most kids will keep an eye on your drawing too, and this way you can gently introduce certain objects or suggest relations or emotions.

Obviously the method is particularly challenging if the child doesn't like to draw in the first place, and you might also find it difficult to find the one-on-one time for a full hour every week, but it's a really powerful tool!

Example

# Put the sky on top of the ocean

Outdoor impressions on paper

Age:      4-12 approx.
Group:   1-5
Purpose: Experience the big shapes and how to
             harness them

When painting outdoors, en plein air, the atmosphere of
the "room" is suddenly everything. All senses are at play
here and perhaps the weather makes it difficult to keep the
pictures dry or free of sand and dust blowing in the wind.

Go to the largest body of water you can find in your area
and paint it. Large watercolour paper blocks are suitable
but less will do. Talk about the horizon line and let the
children find it. Then help the younger ones to draw the line
across the paper with a pencil.

You can talk about small waves and big waves, what they
look like, sound like, what colour the water really is. Make
the children think and observe a bit before they begin.
Allow them to paint with their imagination as well. Tall
waves and sea monsters in the local park makes for interesting conversations after all.

One way of painting is to use crayons first and then water-colour on top of that. It's an interesting blending style.

**TIP**

Try to position yourselves as high as possible to the water. Otherwise all the children see is a narrow strip of water and a lot of sky.

Bring food, water and waterproof pads to sit on.

# Evaluate the process

Whether you set goals or have a vision for the process itself, you probably want to evaluate your efforts at some point. This of course goes for all areas of your work with the children, but you can actually tap into the creative fountain and let the children paint your evaluation for you!

These are broad brushstrokes, I know, but you *can* use drawings and paintings in a simple way to document and from that evaluate your work.

A quite common way to evaluate is to only address it at the end of the process or activity. Taking photos of the kids' art exhibit on the wall and trying to look back at how it went. But if you're aware of *how* you want to evaluate before you even begin the process, you'll be able to document the process itself and adjust along the way.

One creative way to evaluate is to ask the children to draw something in the beginning, about half way and again in the end. For example: if you're teaching the children about the weather, ask them to draw the current weather every day or once a week depending on your timeframe. Look for progress in details such as wind direction or maybe temperature indicators like warm gloves or shorts, or whatever your focus might be.

You can't measure this sort of progress accurately, but you'll probably get a strong indicator if you're on the right track or not. Are the kids learning? Do they remember what they experienced a week ago or what I told them about melting ice an hour ago?

Using this method could also make you aware of any by-products of your process. Evolvement in other areas you hadn't foreseen.

# Painting with 1-3 year olds

Painting sometimes gets a little easier when the children get older, but here are a few things to keep in mind when creating with the youngest.

## Producing
Sometimes the child is practising to produce, not to draw. Paper after paper with only a few scribbles on each. This is very natural. Use cheap photocopy paper and save it for later use as notepaper or raw materials in papier-mâché.

## Colour selection
When preparing for a painting activity, pick only a few colours that you know will look good together. Present only one or two colours at a time or rotate them around the table. It depends on the chosen medium, but most paints will blend into murky grey and brown when wet. Consider drying time in between colours and perhaps choose wide brushes for the light colours and a smaller one for the dark afterwards.

## Timeframe
Paint only for 5-15 minutes at a time. The attention span of 1-3 year olds is usually not much longer.

## Simple shapes

If you want to assign subjects then go for simple shapes. Lines one day. Circles the next day. Some children in this age group might be able to draw *around* something – a rock or a toy. The ability to combine shapes in a more controlled manner usually comes around 3-4 years, although some kids get it much sooner.

## Display and exhibit

Children this age aren't really focusing on what's on the walls way above their heads. Consider displaying their artwork on the floor. Obviously the paint must be dry and you might want to keep an eye on anyone crawling on the pictures and covering them with drool, but at least you're exhibiting the artworks where both children and parents can see and appreciate them.

## When is the picture done?

You know the situation where the child is drawing and drawing and the picture gets darker and darker. You want to stop the child but not limit it either. Who're you to decide if the picture is done? One approach is to distinguish between tasks initiated by you and drawings initiated by the child itself. When you have set the parameters of the activity, it's okay to stop when the task is completed. Otherwise sit on your hands and let the kid draw!

# How to interpret a child's creation

It's almost impossible to look at a child's painting or drawing without making assumptions and interpret it one way or the other: "Isn't mommy looking a bit angry in that picture?"

But we should be careful with that. What we see is sometimes random marks and the result of motor skills not yet

fully developed. Sometimes it's simply the result of a creative, joyful outburst. A heavy use of black paint doesn't necessarily mean anger or depression, but could be a fondness for the contrast and strong expression it makes.

Research into colour psychology indicates that the way colour affects us is largely dependent on cultural factors, previous experiences and associations with particular colours. By transferring our adult mutual symbolic understanding of colours to the child's world, we unintentionally come to see the child as an object that is *becoming* an adult (a "real person") and not a human *being* in itself. The wide difference between *becoming* and *being* is a century long philosophical discussion.

We also tend to interpret a child's creation as a product instead of considering the process. Observe the child during the creative process. Then allow the child to tell you afterwards what the drawing is about and how it makes them feel. This ties in to some of the ideas in Andreasens Drawing-Talking method.

Sometimes you find the meaning behind the art together…

# Be bold and colourful

Lead the way and show children that the crayon is mightier than the sword. More greasy but mightier.

You're their role model and must show them how to explore and express themselves in visual media. By taking the first steps *with* the children you encourage curiosity, adventure and the ability to take action. It's your responsibility to learn them to think laterally and paint outside the lines sometimes.

When you fail to draw that dinosaur and it looks like a sack of potatoes, the children learn that it's okay not to succeed at first and that you ultimately decide what *your* dinosaur should look like.

Go crazy with every colour on the palette, feel the paint and let it inspire you. Truly explore the possibilities with the children.

You can do this!

# If you want to know more


Andreasen, A. K. (2011). *Tegne-samtale-metoden.* Frydenlund <- in Danish

Cropley, A. (2020). Creativity-focused Technology Education in the Age of Industry 4.0. *Creativity Research Journal 32*:2, 184-191.

Dunn, R. & Dunn, K. (1978). *Teaching Students Through Their Individual Learning Styles*. Allyn & Bacon.

Gardner, H. (2006). *Multiple Intelligences: New Horizons in Theory and Practice*. Basic Books.

Ross, M. (2011). *Cultivating the Arts in Education and Therapy*. Routledge.

Stern, D. N. (1985). *The Interpersonal World of the Infant.* Routledge.

Thornton, L. & Brunton, P. (2014). *Understanding the Reggio Approach*. Routledge.

Wadsworth, B. J. (1976). *Piaget's Theory of Cognitive Development*. Addison-Wesley Longman Ltd.

# Thank you

Anne-Cathrine, emotional support

Molly and Lasse, illustrations

Alina, linguistic support

Children, co-workers, students and mentors
from various daycare centres and colleges